Copyright © 2022 by Cristina Umpfenbach-Smyth

All rights reserved.

A Come Again production.

Cover Design by Lisa Knox, OMNi Design

SHOUT OUT TO VIVIAN

Our past has made memories
we'll hold onto forever,
We've now made the future
our newest endeavor.

SHOUTS&WHISPERS AND OTHER NOISES

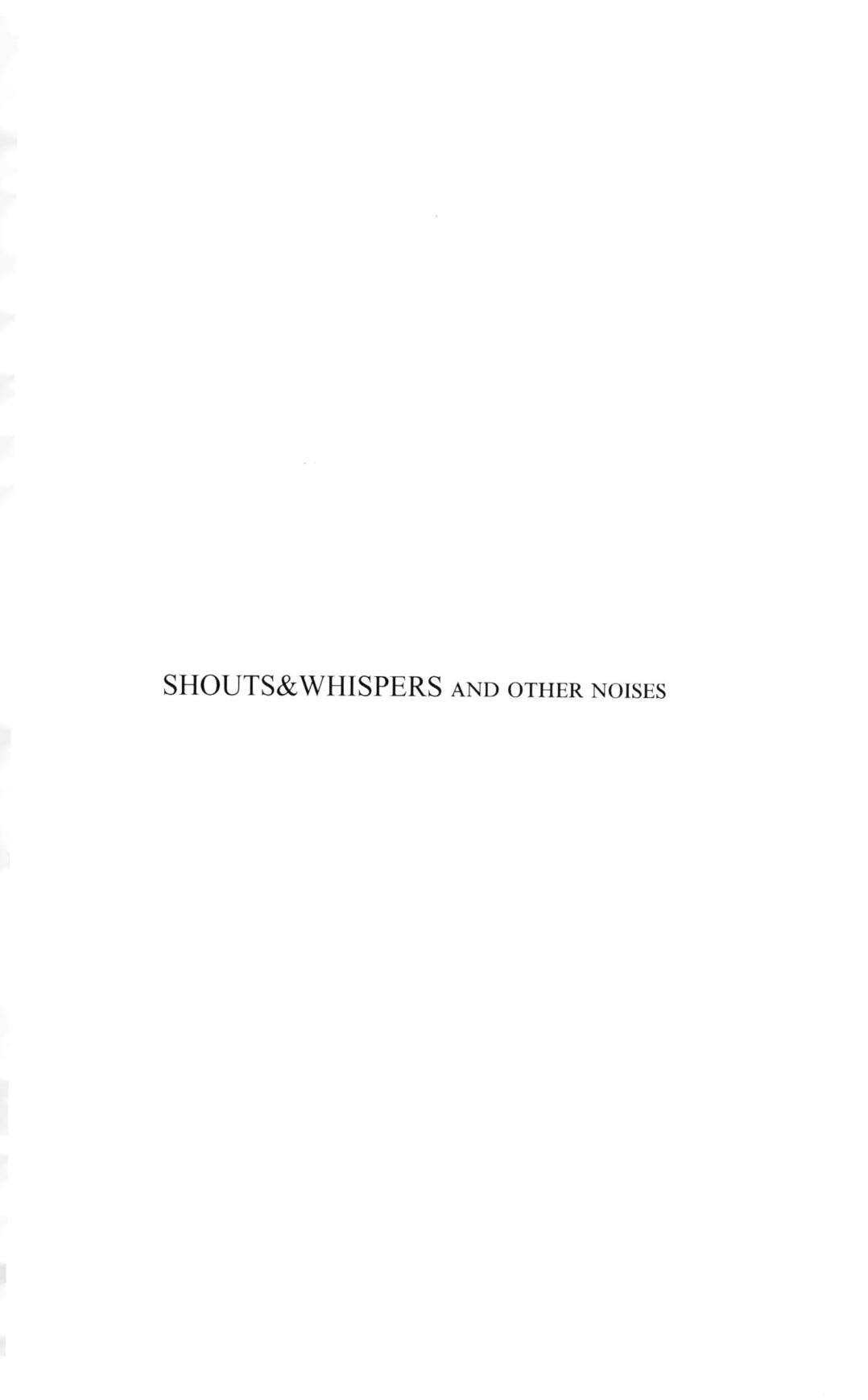

Thank you all my friends who have encouraged me to do this! You know who you are!

Special thanks to Joseph Galante, who did all the grunt work, and for holding my hand!

Table of Contents

HOW LONG IS Now?..1
ZEITGEIST...2
ROGUE WAVE..4
DISCORD..5
WHAT'S LEFT BEHIND..6
BLUE/YELLOW DOGS...7
DARK PLACES..8
FINALE...9
AGNOSTIC...10
LEAVING..11
SLOW BREATHING...12
WALKING WITH MOTHER...13
MY FATHER...14
TIDE OF BLUE...15
PETER...16
HER WISH..17
DAFFODIL DAWN...18
SEASIDE AFTERNOON..19
MOUNTAIN DAWN...20
CREPUSCULE..21
AFTER...22
NIGHT STORM AT SEA..23
MELANCHOLY..24
SUMMERCAMP MEMORIES...25
WINTER STORM WITHOUT YOU...26
HEAT...27
UPTOWN SUMMERNIGHT..28
TROPHY WIFE...29
EXPECTATION...30

HOT SAUCE.	31
BACKWATER LIFE.	32
THROUGH A LENSE SHARPLY.	33
A LITTLE NIGHT MUSIC.	34
NURSERY RHYME.	35
KALEIDOSCOPE.	36
DICHOTOMY.	37
ALWAYS MORE.	38
CAUGHT.	39
REMEMBER.	40
ALL THERE IS.	41
BLESSING OR CURSE?	42
WHEN I THINK OF YOU.	43
JASMINE NOIR.	44
IN THE HOUR OF PAN.	45
BLOSSOM.	46
DEMENTIA (1)	47
DEMENTIA (2)	48
HALCYON DAYS.	49
HOURGLASS. (MISTRAL)	51
BETWEEN THE HOURS.	53
ORTOLAN EATERS. (La Belle Epoque)	55
UPTOWN GIRL	56
AFTERNOON IN THE SERAGLIO.	57
LETTING GO.	58
BEADING WORDS.	59
BLUES	60
FULL FORWARD.	61
FREE.	62
ORIGINAL.	63

You can shout through your art, through your clothes, through your ideas, through your silence, through your stance! Instead of shouting through your mouth, chose the above elegant ways of shouting!
Mehmet Murat ildan

The words of the prophets are written on subway walls and tenement halls, and whispered in the sound of silence.
Paul Simon

There is nothing more harrowing than the deadly hush with the feel of a great noise around it.
Jessie Douglas Kerruish (The Underlying Monster).

HOW LONG IS Now?

I live the NOW,
urinate a stream,
asparagus scented piss.
I am not sure how long the NOW.
Enough to seize the day,
or two? Live them one at a time?
NOW is a shelter from past transgressions
and future deeds.
I like my yesterdays,
my to-morrows, fraught as they may be
with faulty memories and wishful thinking.

ZEITGEIST.

Darkness shouts.
Against a canvass of blackness,
deaf people dance
with succubae and incubuses.
Tiny gymnasts
balance on sharp edged swords
in le cirque du soleil
under a moonless sky.

Grimm's tales of baked children
and hungry wolves play out.
On a runway starving women show
the latest fashion in cardinal red.
The Grinch stole my green silk Balenciaga gown,
gave it to the frog prince.
Sleeping beauty is just a junkie.
She had too much of all of it.

Hermes glass slippers are sold
only to a few deserving Cinderellas,
trophy wives of mummified kings.
What they really deserve is not on the menu,
just le plat du jour of ortolans.
The three pigs are out of breath,
not enough air for a blow job.

Rose colored glasses take on a nasty hue
of watered-down blood.
Bottle green is not the color du jour,
rather a bile color
with tint of pus yellow.
There is a storm brewing,
a tsunami rising, earth shakes,
red lava licks down a mountain.

Cristina Umpfenbach-Smyth

Destiny, fate, Apocalypse?
A voice whispers:
Put up a shield of bright,
paint with bold strokes of
earthen tones.
Mold vessels to hold the morning dew,
catch rays of sun
in a glass glockenspiel.
Hum the world, sing life, hope.

ROGUE WAVE.

A wave of uncertainty
hits the quicksand beach.

Recedes, builds higher, stronger,
draws sand from under
feet grasping for a hold.

It carries sharp edged shells
of broken promises,
shattered dreams;

and Jedermann's straw hat,
the one he lost on the beach
a few years back.

Cristina Umpfenbach-Smyth

DISCORD.

There is no roundness in this edgy day.
No harmony in tune.

Dadaesque shadows play on walls,
hurried footfalls without echoes.

At night, a square moon swims in the river,
holding its light.

The Sun rises,
hiding under the bridge.

WHAT'S LEFT BEHIND.

At times he misses his leg.
He imagines it hanging in a tree
in the jungle of Vietnam,
or maybe it fell to the ground,
a bloody mess.

Now picked clean,
fibula and tibia shiny white,
foot broken into hundred pieces
strewn about.

He thinks about farmers plowing the land
of a denuded jungle,
discarding bones into a ditch.
Mass grave of lost parts.

He thinks had he lost his head instead,
somewhere, someone may be standing,
holding his skull. Like Hamlet,
pondering a question.

Cristina Umpfenbach-Smyth

BLUE/YELLOW DOGS.

Two dogs fight over a bone,
drink melted snow from muddy puddles.
A purple stuffed animal in debris
brightens the grayscale of destruction.

The bone, remnant of a limb
flung into the rubble
of explosive collapse.
A body carted to the grave
missing an arm or leg.

The dogs are thin and hungry.
They shiver in the cold.
Somewhere a child is missing their pet.
The dogs are waiting patiently,
hold hope for someone to return.

DARK PLACES.

Deep pockets in a velvet coat
lined with razor blades
night trains without destination
rubber band snap back
to all the wrong places
I should not have been.

FINALE

stewing in anguish
with a dash of angst
in a brew of anxiety,

I hide
behind the facades
of Potemkin villages,
behind the curtains
of the theatre
of the absurd.

Godot is not coming.

AGNOSTIC.

An altar of whatever,
chalice of self-deception,
ciborium with chards of glass,
chorales of hollow promises,
choir out of tune,
display of shoddy emotion
preached by forked tongues.
I do not
worship this God.

Cristina Umpfenbach-Smyth

LEAVING.

Naked windows
host opaque reflections.
Impulses keep vigil
in this house of cards.

Without spring or stitch,
address or stamp
there is nothing to hold to.
No clingable mass.

Discontent growls.
Memories zigzag.
A legacy spawned unknowingly.
No one waves good bye.

SLOW BREATHING

nothing delineated
nothing marked,
no highs,
no lows.
Fluid, streaming
blending days into nights,
nights merge into days,
the names of days matter not.
Jumble of weeks turn into months.

I am here,
breathing.

Cristina Umpfenbach-Smyth

WALKING WITH MOTHER.

My list, necessities to be gotten
at the mall.
Flannel sheets by Martha S.,
preferably blue.
Underwear, Hanes,
regular cut, white.
A jar of overpriced crème
for lines which disappear
only to my decreasing sight.
Last, a dash to the Ladies Room;
Nordstrom calls it "Women's Lounge",
comforting in case you are not a Lady.
On the way there I stop dead
by a pair of boots
just like my mother had.
Emotional hurricane.
Remembering mother's stride.
I leave with them.

MY FATHER.

My father towers.
Leather coat
black against white snow.
The scull on his hat
does not scare me.
He has lightning on his lapel.
He kisses me good bye.

When the sirens hush
and the flags fall,
he returns.

Not as tall,
no leather coat,
no pedestal.
It is summer now.
He holds my hand
as we walk through the rubble
of his life.

Cristina Umpfenbach-Smyth

TIDE OF BLUE.
(for my sister Carola, a stroke victim)

The world is grey beyond the rain,
drops stream down the windowpane.
a smell of coffee in the room.
She once had coffee in a place
with yellow curtains.

She had a dress of bright blue silk,
she swam in seas of otherworldly blue,
blue was the music in her soul,
blue mountains under sunny skies,
blueberries and blue birds in flight.

Where have they gone those shades of blue?
Like puzzle pieces lost in space
now rushing back,
blue crashing waves
that hurt her mind.

She blinks.

She watched rain.
Drops stream down the windowpane.
A smell of coffee in the room.
She once had coffee in a place
With yellow curtains.

PETER.
(for my brother who died too young fighting his demons.)

I look for you behind facades,
among sand castles claimed by the tide,
on crooked streets among the neon lights.

I find you

hiding back stage
in the theatre of the absurd.
Give me your hand my brother,
walk center stage with me.

where

the end of the rainbow is a toy box
full of paper mâché rhinoceroses,
and eagles live in cuckoo clocks
among glass spiders in gossamer webs.

You are safe here from the
bald soprano's siren song

for a while

let's be young again,
laughing ourselves into tears,
dancing, singing, believing
in forever.

And when you leave again,
remember brother,

I will always find you.

Cristina Umpfenbach-Smyth

HER WISH.
(for my sister Lilo)

When air lies still upon my lips,
I am gone. Clean this corpse.
Fold this cadaver into a sheet,
carry it to the hill behind the house.
Lay it onto the stone
among the Manzanita brush.
Unfold me, a gift of carrion.
Watch buzzards gather in the sky.

Sing, dance, drink wine.
Conjure me from your memories,
thus let me dance among you.
In a year's time gather the
rain washed, sun bleached bones,
grind them to scatter on the land.
You may remember then,
I loved the purple lilac most.

DAFFODIL DAWN.

Powder sugar frost o
on roofs.
Cold shivers over the road.
Under barren land
somethings stirs,
awakens,
slowly unfolds.

SEASIDE AFTERNOON.

Rush of waves, pulsating.
sun warm on my skin
awakens longings,
for somewhere, something,
undefined.

Memories are scented shadows,
packages to be unwrapped
another time.
Melancholy mood drifts
into the afternoon.

MOUNTAIN DAWN.

As morning slowly grows
to early light,
ochre and burnt sienna sweep the hills.
Hazy purple fills the valleys.
Green awakens.
A touch of golden sun
makes promises.

Pale crescent moon
hangs in the sky
discarded by the waning night.

CREPUSCULE.

Sun fades pink and gold
into a liquid sky
dark spreads under trees
stealing the last rays of light
stillness tenses
at first sound of night.

AFTER.

Storm is gone.
All is quiet now.
Denuded trees stretch.
A colorful carpet covers the lawn.
A lone leave shivers
On an empty branch,
Counting the silence.

NIGHT STORM AT SEA.

Sunset slides over the horizon,
leaves strands of pink. Sky swallows stars.
We float in eerie calm.
Nerves electrify,
body tenses in anticipation, excitement, fear.
Harnesses vibrate to the hum of stanchions,
halyards strain, the steaming masthead light
barely reflects in the expanse
of the obsidian night.

An overture of rain pellets the flesh,
lightning flashes rhythmic strobes,
clouds play percussion out of tune.
We plunge ahead through overhanging crests,
into the troughs voracious appetite.
Feet melt into the creaking deck,
hands wrestle with the helm,
salt crusted lips swear,
screams turn to voiceless laughs.

The storm abates,
breathes upon us one more time,
sprays farewell,
leaves to thunderous applause.

MELANCHOLY.

Chewy chocolate fudge of sadness
on rainy days or balmy moonlight nights.
It tastes of fog and feels like Santa Ana winds.
It smells of jasmine, bread no longer baked,
and mother's coffee.

Such blue deep longings
for songs not heard and colors never seen,
sweet kisses never shared with lovers never met.
It whispers thoughts I never dared or had.
Haunting sweet pain.

And then it leaves as quietly as it came.

Cristina Umpfenbach-Smyth

SUMMERCAMP MEMORIES.
(my first love)

These are sad goodbyes.
We maintain posture,
words remain silent
behind smiles.

We dare not kiss away the barriers,
the circumstances.
We are not bold and strong enough.

These are sad good-byes.
Our sandcastle swept away
by the tide. Our kites are folded.
We shake the blanket.
Hopes and expectation fall into the sand,
with a few blades of grass from where we laid
in the dunes and dreamed.

The beach is empty now but for an old couple
walking a dog.

WINTER STORM WITHOUT YOU.

Strong winds make rain dance on the roof.
High heels perform passionate flamencos.
The windows weep pear shaped tears.
Fog wraps the house in dirty rags.

You died
Twelve months,
four weeks,
three days
ago

Your aunt said "he's in a better place."
What better place than here, with me?
Your uncle said "it was his time."
I saw no expiration date.

I feel no anger, no denial and accept
that you are gone. The deep ache in me,
the painful rise and fall of memories
will never cease.

I hold your favorite shirt, fold it under my head.
It smells of you and sea and sand and sweat.
Across the front it reads:
"keep the daily bread, give me the wine and cheese!"

I hear you laugh and swallow tears.

Cristina Umpfenbach-Smyth

HEAT.

Shadows of the outside world
filter through a muslin curtain,
unmoving in oppressive heat.

She sprawls on sweat soaked sheets.
Fan clanks and chops her pastel world,
imaginary calm and peace.
A house of cards.

Her scented candles melt.
Her mantra out of rhythm.
A step away, the abyss,
Razor-sharp blood rimmed.

UPTOWN SUMMERNIGHT.

Ten years, his gestures still unfamiliar,
the way he holds his cup,
his laugh, needs, wants.
He gives me flowers,
red carnations, I like yellow roses.
At night he reaches for me,
his arm around my waist,
draws me close.
He falls into a deep contended sleep.

I huddle on the fire escape.
Oppressive heat, uptown summer night
sticks to my skin.
A pockmarked moon melts into a water tower.
Across the alley a television strobes blue.
Sirens repeat themselves.
Stink rides on heavy air.
Music drifts, seeps into me, makes me rock,
I want a cigarette, a drink, a fuck.

A woman screams below.
I feel the sound. Stomach rises into my throat.
The scar across my face burns hot.
Familiar pain rises.
I crawl back,
close the window, draw the drapes.
The fan labors against stagnant air.
I slide into bed,
into safety, still unfamiliar.

Cristina Umpfenbach-Smyth

TROPHY WIFE.

Ethereal beauty,
she moves with grace.
Firm breasts barely raise her sheath.
Perfect smile,
feet a fetishist delight.
Men envy him
his wife,
his collection of cubist masters.

He looks at her asleep.
Moonlight plays on her face,
unkindly casts sharp angles.
Her skeleton frame barely
raises the sheets.

He dreams Rubenesque,
pendulous breasts,
nourishing milk laden,
round meaty buttocks,
eager hips to meet his thrust,
swollen pink labia,
welcoming deep moist escape.
He knew it once.

He moans.
She moves slightly.

EXPECTATION.

Her contour softened now,
black lace teddy with snap away crotch,
never worn,
hidden under white cotton undies.
There was a time when she hoped.

Ten years of his grunting bulk,
she still got expectations.
Lovers emerge from a handheld shower head.
Some soft, some rough.
They lick, kiss and fuck to her liking
until she shudders.

She slips into bed smiling.
He turns away
thinking of pole dancers
in red lace teddies with snap away crotches.

HOT SAUCE.

You never told me
What it is,
that secret ingredient
you add
to our emotional highs,
that which takes my breath away,
binds us together.
That which spices our nights
and makes for happy days.
You never told me
that secret ingredient,
that dash of something,
like a shake of hot sauce into
an ordinary stew,
short of burning the mouth.

BACKWATER LIFE.

A pool, a pond, discarded, rejected
from the river's flow.
Stagnant, murky, foul.
Willows recoil,
guard their graceful branches
from touching the surface.
Even Catfish do not dwell here.
Water birds do not visit.

Backwater.

But when the moon is full
and hangs just so,
it shimmers quicksilver.
The willows sway like praying ghost,
A nigh bird glides over the surface.
And when the Jasmin blooms
its scent pervades the air,
masking the stench.

Then, for a moment,
from the cabin on the bank,
she sees beauty.
She looks at him,
holding that threadbare bag
of broken promises,
the only thing they ever owned.
And she holds hope.

Cristina Umpfenbach-Smyth

THROUGH A LENSE SHARPLY.

Colors bright
under the midday sun,
green, red,
orange, yellow
a perfect picture,
a perfect angle.
Earthen tone tribal cloth
draped around her
against a bright blue sky,
billows in the breeze
which carries sand
over the parched expanse
that is her life.
She sings softly,
swaying,
waving away flies
on the face
of her starving child.

A LITTLE NIGHT MUSIC.

Geisha moon over a crumbled chimney;
breeze bends graceful reeds
surviving in a dirt patch.
Greyscale corner of the forlorn,
barely tolerated,
invisible.

A woman in a cardboard box
gestures to the golden sphere.
Dirty hands flutter like butterflies.
She hums despair.
Abandoned, Cio Cio San
smokes her poison.

NURSERY RHYME.

Black silhouettes in shadow boxes sway,
think of escape.
Marionettes, strings broken,
lifeless puppets,
think of freedom.
Unarmed tin soldiers
ride headless rocking horses.
The music box skips every other note.

The children have left a long time ago.

Silhouettes in black limousines,
bloated with power,
pull strings of marionettes
in a dance macabre.
Blindfolded soldiers die in foreign places.
Headless horses of the apocalypse
trample freedom
to the tune of greed.

The children have grown up.

KALEIDOSCOPE.

The first time her thoughts left, she enjoyed their take off;
streaking across the expanse of her mind like a Persoid meteor shower,
brightening the darkness of her dreams.

Later, when they bounce off perimeters of awareness,
like squash balls hitting the court's wall, she holds her throbbing head
caught in the deafening sound.

The edge is hiding someplace.

She walks, carefully, setting foot before foot,
arms stretched holding her balance.
A tight rope walker nauseated by the thought of freefall into the void.

Drugs pull her slowly into a comatose sleep.
She wakes, finds her thoughts scattered, scoops tiny pieces of colored glass into a kaleidoscope. Slowly turning the display into radiant patterns,
she only sees pieces of broken glass.

DICHOTOMY.

After the steel's poke
warm embrace
wear a mantle of stars,
a crown of endorphin glow,
bath in sublime calm.

The wanting in the veins
grows fangs and claws,
waits with a hollow freeze,
beckons with the trapeze,
swing high

The low waits, patiently.
There is no net.

ALWAYS MORE.

You always

had more answers than I had questions.
They zig zagged, dazzled, left the
question mark confused.

You always

had more needs than I had giving,
Tentacles probing my orifices,
Left me in joyless surrender.

You always

had more notes than our tune could carry.
Hanging from a broken clef
our song perished with the clap of percussion.

Cristina Umpfenbach-Smyth

CAUGHT.

Panic and fear avoid me.
Conquered and done with
in bunkers and dungeons.

But the other,
the one that hides in daylight,
the one that muddies the creek
drowns my reflection,

THAT ONE

sends whisper thin fog,
obscures clarity,
catches with silken threads.

A silver cocoon
I hang in the web of anxiety.

REMEMBER.

I stroll through sunlit days of memories,
sounds, scents and textures.
Vistas, aromas of my yesterdays.
The purple lilac's scent, fireplace dreams,
gentle touches and passionate embrace.
I walk the meadows, forests, city streets,
the ocean shores of my remembrance.
I greet familiar faces, embrace friends.

 I enter crepuscule, hasten my step,
 leave behind the setting sun's display,
 pass into a darkened hidden space
to mournful chants of faceless choirs.
I run the gauntlet of forgotten anguish,
pain, loss. Struggle through thorny thickets,
landscapes of quicksand and mirages,
lost loves and punches of betrayals.

Breathless I gasp for air,

exhale the shadows,
inhale the light,
and breathe.

Cristina Umpfenbach-Smyth

ALL THERE IS

I search parts of me, find
cracks filled with illusions,
streak of anger running
like a murky stream.
Empty spaces of forgotten
days.

Me,

suspended between
vernal equinoxes
and solstices.
Outbound, EDT unknown.
Carpe Noctem!

BLESSING OR CURSE?

In this silent room
darkness shifts.
Shadow conjure memories,
I feel the music
spicy on my tongue,
bells, violins and tambourines.

We were new to each other,
caught in a joyous crowd
of Romani people,
as they carry the statues
of the Black Marias to the sea.
In this place in Camargue.

We had our fortunes read
by a black-haired woman.
She tied our hands together
with a red ribbon. We laughed.
And then came fall,
And called for reason.

We parted ways.
Now it is May again,
I feel you close to me
In this dark silent room
I smell the sea and jasmine.
I kept that ribbon
blessing or curse?

Cristina Umpfenbach-Smyth

WHEN I THINK OF YOU.

When I think of you
I enter a backwater
unaffected by rising tides.
I pass overhanging branches of memories;
barely see the psychedelic rubbish.

When I think of you,
No address or stamp,
known inheritor of memories.
Foreign as milk slapping
Against a deck in a still backwater.

JASMINE NOIR.

Moon hides above thick clouds.
Jasmine's blooms, virgin white.
Dark seductive scent
pervades the air,
night weighs, a heavy blanket.

Candles flicker in rhythm with our breaths.
Your fingertip traces my spine,
draws a question mark on the small of my back.
Somewhere a tune plays,
"out of my skin."

There was no moon that night of
unanswered questions
and dark jasmine.

IN THE HOUR OF PAN.

In the old stone house on the hill
among the olive groves,
is a room where we rest,
shielded from the midday heat
in the hour of Pan.

Cicadas cease their cacophony,
breezes are still among the trees
as time hangs in the balance of the day.
The sound of an imaginary flute
drifts our way.

A cat jumps on the window sill
leads us into another place,
where love runs strong and deep
and stays unquestioned,
while we sleep.

BLOSSOM.

In the long evening silence
night gathers darkness.
Vanilla scented moon rolls over cedars,
stirs longing for by-gone days.

I planted a bed of Forget-you flowers,
icy white hearts.
As I look for them,
I find bright blue Forget-me-not.

In the long evening silence
lavender clouds
ride the breeze into the ending day.
I wonder, can this heart still blossom?

Cristina Umpfenbach-Smyth

DEMENTIA (1)

A wasteland,
deep dry well
holds
muzzled thoughts,
stifled tongues,
futile actions.
Parchment thin
dried
remnants from
another time,
unsalvageable,
forever lost.

DEMENTIA (2)

words drift
aimless
broken
brushstrokes
meaningless
blotches
in muddied
timeless
days of incomprehension.

HALCYON DAYS.

Facades rise in memory.
Paint peels, marble columns lean.
Rain drowns piazzas.
The bridge of sighs moans in sorrow.
Windows stare sightless into the past.
Cats remember.....

…….............. the rustling of silk,
jeweled hands tending morsels;
magenta robes, the caped,
flash of daggers in starlight;
the glory on sun drenched Sundays
when church bells summon the faithful,
morning sun bounces off golden domes,
water shimmers a crisp mother of pearl.

In the white palace, with marble columns,
rich and poor bow to the Republic's justice.
Doges in pointed hats, crimson robes,
cast fate from bejeweled hands.
In Basilicas and stone chapels
priests give absolution, in musty confessional,
hidden behind velvet curtains.
Jews, marked in red hats, hurry to the ghetto.

Sweaty men push a barge with a coffin
draped in gold brocade, blood red roses.
A cross encased with jewels catches the light.
Altar boys swing vessels, incense permeates the air.
High voices intone monotonous chants.
Mourners follow, sway in a rhythm of grief.
Under veils tears streak white chalked faces,
red lips know of secrets.

Celebrants toast a newly wedded couple
with sweet scented deep ruby red wine.
To the sound of flutes and tambourines
pairs spill into the campo for a joyful dance.

They freeze in a moment in silence,
watch the funeral procession,
make the sign of the cross, return to their feast
of rosemary scented boar......
.........now canals choke in mud,
fight ruin in oil slick stagnant waters.
Palazzos put on a false face under layers of peeling paint.
Greedy currents lick at foundations,
slowly swallow remains,
suck them into hostile marshes.

The Campanile rings the hour.

HOURGLASS.   (MISTRAL)

Kayaks pulled on a crescent beach,
between the rocks below the cliffs.
The sea barely licks the sand.
Cicadas incessantly chant.

I stretch in shadowy coolness,
my mind takes a walk.
I find an hourglass in need of sand,
fill it, grain by grain by hand.

Your finger traces my spine
from the nape of my neck
to the small of my back
where you draw a question mark.

Later, in the house on the hill
moonless night brightens stars.
Mimosa trees whisper.
Cats pace nervously.

A sudden burst of air, shutters clank,
turbulence bends trees,
rattles roof tiles,
howls of the unknown.

Your question mark on my back
demands an answer.
I kiss it into your mouth,
We rise and fall with the staccato of Mistral.

Three days it howls, under bright blue skies,
chills the air, boils the sea.
Restless sleep, stormy love,
We live the rhythms.

One morning we wake to stillness.
The sea breathes against the shore.
Cicadas chirp, cats stretch lazily,
trees stand still. The air warm.

We take the kayaks to that spit of beach
between the rocks, below the cliffs.
We rest in shade, we kiss.
I turn the hourglass.

BETWEEN THE HOURS.

Grey stone buildings jumble on the promontory.
White cliffs fall to the sea like bridal veils,
merge with the blue waters of the summer season.
The land lies still, wanting, waiting,
change of season late in coming.

Cisterns are dry, roses wilt.
A black-glad woman walks the garden.
Dry leaves dance suddenly along the path.
Her tongue licks the faint movement of air.
Storm clouds gather in the East.

After Vespers and Compline
the young nun enters her chamber,
opens the window, pushes back heavy panes.
Sea fuses into obsidian sky.
Starlight dims behind racing clouds.

She sheds her habit for a white muslin sheath,
beds down on the narrow cot.
A slight breeze rolls over the window sill,
continues through the room, playfully
caresses the woman's fee, licks her cheek.

A stronger gust follows,
pushed under her dress,
waves up her inner thighs, caresses her belly,
rubs the stubby hair of her shorn head.
Her toes curl, knuckles turn white.

The storm comes full and strong,
carries dried leaves of roses,
scent of salty sea, fecund fields.
Her sheath pushes up around her waist,
an offer to a pagan god.

Window shutters clank in protest,
waves crash against the rocky shore.
Clouds shed their load of heavy rain.
The virgin sleeps, limbs askew
until the hour of Aurora and Lauds.

ORTOLAN EATERS. (La Belle Epoque)

Fattened birds in gilded cages,
blinded, still sing.
Blood red roses in crystal vases,
Champagne in silver buckets.
A feast for Monsieur and his bride.
He, prosperous man sans titre,
debauched flaneur, she virgin, pauper princess.

Carriages arrive, spill ladies and gents,
Mademoiselle and her widow mother,
Monsieur and his entourage.
Heads bow under white linen coverings,
silver bowls placed, birds intact,
scalded alive in boiling water, sucked, chewed,
release their essence of Provence.

Mademoiselle, chokes under her cover,
reminded that eating ortolans may be
the least repulsive event of her nuptials.

UPTOWN GIRL

She rests on the small bed
with the Afghan his grandmother knitted.
A cactus tries to survive on the sill
of a single window.

She watches him, amused,
as he opens the jar of spaghetti sauce
with serious concentration.
The paste boils in the pot
on the single hotplate.
It is their meal when she visits.

She has come to like it
with the cardboard cheese from a plastic bag.
He will try to kiss her again,
but she will not allow intimacy.

She brought pears.
She taught him how to eat them,
unpeeled and whole
from between her thighs,
in little bites and licks
until she is satisfied.

Her husband was annoyed
when she started laughing
as he ate his favorite dessert
at their usual haunt:
pear poached in port wine
with heavy cream.

Cristina Umpfenbach-Smyth

AFTERNOON IN THE SERAGLIO.

Light flutters through lattice covers
on high windows,
shatters golden on marble floors.
The Odalisque stretches lazily,
undulating creamy flesh
barely covered in a white gauzy sheath.
The low divan covered in purple silk.
Fragrant yellow flower petals
float in kaleidoscopic mosaic fountains.

She sinks into the pillows,
uncovers her breast,
stiffens her ripe nipples with wetted fingers.
Her bored expression changes.
Her pale hand starts exploring
the labia of her sleeping companion.
The young slave wakens aroused.
Sinks into knowing flesh. Clitoris stiffened.
They take their time, explore crevasses.
Fingers penetrate, rub
their buttocks lift and sink,
breasts are tongued.

The Eunuch watches them,
waits for a sign to join. In anticipation
he flickers his eager orphidian tongue..

LETTING GO.

Toes once curled in pleasure
now curl in pain.
Soft spots harden,
what was firm dissolves.

Mind clings to clock,
Heart aches for last caress,
Spirit ready to soar.

Cristina Umpfenbach-Smyth

BEADING WORDS.

Words are gathered in trays.
Sorted by color and lengths,
all shades and hues imaginable.
Commas and points come brass and silver,
question and exclamation marks in gold,
accents, aigu, grave, tréma and circonflexe of iron.

She fashions words into strands,
strung like beads,
none pleases her.

The waste bin overflows
with discards of her making.
She sighs, picks up a question mark,
starts anew
hopes for an answer.

BLUES

Our end was pre-ordained,
a weeklong one- night- stand.
I listen to your footfall down the hall.
I turn and there is Blues, next to the bed,
velvet wings folded behind a gargoyle head.

He waved,
"Come here, lay down go light a cigarette".
"no, I don't smoke" I said.
Blues shrugs, "then get a drink instead".
I settled on the bed.
The sheets still smelled of us and I of you.
I grabbed a beer, wash down a chocolate bar.
I closed my eyes.
Blues jumped into my chest
sandpapered my heart
to music,
until it bled.

Cristina Umpfenbach-Smyth

FULL FORWARD.

My colors are too bold
for shallow praises
and bowing to your needs for
miseries companion.
If you can't meet me eye to eye,
unadorned and raw,
back off!
I do not live vicariously
through others dreams,
pain and loss.
I face my own privations.

Full forward.

FREE.

Defying gravity
floating
relaxed
limbs askew
unattached
the puppet master's hands
empty of strings.

ORIGINAL.

I do not want to be identified
by this and as that,
labeled, stamped, confirmed,
mixed and matched
into form, standards, statistics.
I want to unravel
like an old sweater
that has seen better days.
Row by row,
I follow the unraveled thread
to the floor,
gather them into a new skein
to weave a tapestry
of my own.

ABOUT THE AUTHOR.

Cristina Umpfenbach-Smyth grew up in Frankfurt/Main, Germany. After she graduated from Lyceum she took a summer job in the South of France before heading to hotel management and hospitality school in Switzerland. As fate, or luck, would have it, she met her husband on the Island of Porquerolles and stayed in Provence for a number of years, avoiding the harsh winters in Switzerland.

Cristina became a staff writer for a German travel magazine and freelanced for others, which afforded her many opportunities to travel within Europe, the Balkans, the Middle East and North Africa.

After a few years living on her own schedule, enjoying the barefoot live, she decided to return to Frankfurt, but not for long. She travelled on holiday to New York City and liked it so much that she stayed there, living in Manhattan (Greenwich Village) and pursuing a career.

Cristina is now settled in the Pacific Northwest, in Washington State across from Portland, Oregon.

She translates various materials, including books, from German to English and vis versa.

She still travels, enjoys gardening, cooking for friends, winetasting and adventures as they come along.

A NIGHTWING PUBLICATION 2015

harmonies & discords

cristina umpfenbach-smyth

Cristina Umpfenbach-Smyth's harmonies unfold as concise, crystalline miniatures, encapsulating natural states as though a Mary Oliver vision had been distilled for a haiku consciousness. But place her in a vector of discord, whether over breast cancer or the inability of others to forgive, and she will apply that same distillation to searing examinations of exquisitely-defined moments of fear and sorrow. By offering this yin and yang in a single volume of poetry, Umpfenbach-Smyth serves up the ideal balanced diet.

~ Loring Wirbel/Poet/Journalist

Made in the USA
Coppell, TX
13 February 2023

12752791R00046